# OLD WARDOUR

WILTSHIRE

Brian K. Davison OBE
BA, FSA, MIFA

*When first built for John, the fifth Lord Lovel, in the last years of the fourteenth century, Old Wardour was one of the most daring, innovative and beautiful residences in Britain. The Arundell family, who acquired Wardour in 1570, recognised the quality of the old house and took immense care to preserve its character in the course of their refurbishments.*

*Even though part of the house was irretrievably ruined during the English Civil War, it continued to exert a powerful hold on the imagination. When the Arundells moved into New Wardour in 1776, the old house became the eye-catching centrepiece of a fashionable Romantic landscape – an historical pleasure park, created for the private enjoyment of the Arundell family and their guests.*

*Two centuries later, Old Wardour provides a fascinating blend of medieval castle, Elizabethan mansion and Georgian country idyll.*

# ❖ CONTENTS ❖

*Published by English Heritage*
*1 Waterhouse Square, 138-142 Holborn,*
*London EC1N 2ST*
*© English Heritage 1999*
*First published by English Heritage 1999*
*Reprinted 2000, 2005, 2006, 2008*
*Photographs by English Heritage Photographic*
*Unit and copyright English Heritage, unless*
*otherwise stated*

*Edited by Louise Wilson*
*Designed by Derek Lee*
*Printed in England by The Colourhouse*
*C50, 05/08 ISBN 978-1-85074-740-6*

**50% recycled**
This book is printed
on 50% recycled paper

# DESCRIPTION
# AND TOUR

❖

For 250 years, Old Wardour Castle was the imposing residence of two successive noble families, a vivid symbol of their wealth and status.

It was a centre of power and authority, the hub of a great estate, and home to a bustling household of servants. Now it stands deserted amid green lawns and trees, a romantic relic from an earlier and very different age.

This contrast is not accidental. During the eighteenth century the owners of Old Wardour moved to a new house they had built nearby. The ruins of the old castle were made to look more romantic and were surrounded by a natural-looking but entirely artificial parkland. A prehistoric stone circle, a grotto and a tea-house were added to complete what was, in effect, a private historical theme park.

Because of these changes, it is not easy to visualise Wardour when it was the home of its builder, John, fifth Lord Lovel, or Sir Matthew Arundell,

*The imposing ruined front of Old Wardour Castle*

a great Elizabethan connoisseur-collector.

The tour in this guidebook follows the path that would have been taken by visitors to Lord Lovel's newly-finished home in about the year 1400, noting the alterations made later by the Arundell family.

*To begin the tour, it is best to walk across the lawn in front of the house to the information panel which faces the front door.*

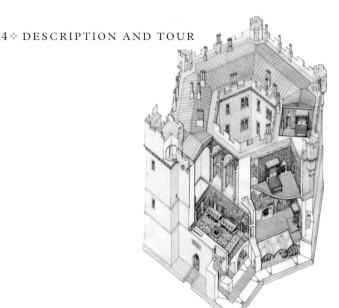

*Cutaway reconstruction drawing by Stephen Conlin, showing the castle in about 1400*

## THE OUTER COURTYARD

The stone wall which encloses the castle grounds, and through which you have entered, was built in the sixteenth century. However, it seems to have followed the line of the original medieval wall, built to protect the great house constructed for Lord Lovel in the last years of the fourteenth century.

In the early eighteenth century, after the house had been abandoned, the grounds remained in use and formal gardens were laid out round the ruins. The present lawns and cedar trees are part of a slightly later garden scheme. Even in the Middle Ages, however, there would have been gardens – possibly round the other side of the house where it was sunnier and more private.

In those days, important visitors to the castle would have come on horseback, winding down a track through the woods. The defensive wall and gatehouse that would have confronted them have been destroyed by later landscaping, which also removed the stables and outhouses that flanked this outer courtyard. The gatehouse was probably at the foot of the wooded slope, behind the later eighteenth-century Grotto: its ruins may even have inspired the shape and appearance of the Grotto.

The front of Lord Lovel's house would originally have been much more warlike in appearance. A threat to his peace was more likely to have come from a peasant revolt than from an invading army: however, his status as a nobleman demanded that his new house should have the appearance of a castle, with portcullis, battlements and turrets.

The harshness of these military precautions was countered by the tall graceful windows of the Great Hall, the fine carvings below the battlements, the exotic six-sided plan of the place, and possibly by the use of white limewash and coloured paint. Lord Lovel's new house was undoubtedly a secure one – but it would also have been instantly recognisable as the luxurious home of a man of immense wealth and the most sophisticated taste.

# ❖ JOHN, FIFTH LORD LOVEL ❖

John Lovel's wealth and status came through marriage. He was a minor baron in his own right, but his marriage to the heiress Maud Holand brought him enormous wealth and a family connection to some of the greatest figures in the land.

By the marriage of their widowed mother to the Prince of Wales, Maud's cousins became the half-brothers of King Richard II. One of them went on to marry a grand-daughter of the old king, Edward III, and became Duke of Exeter: his son became Duke of Surrey. Through his wife's relations, John Lovel thus came into contact with one of the most luxurious and cosmopolitan courts in Europe.

Richard II was not a great feudal warrior like his father

BRITISH LIBRARY (Harley 7026 f4v)

and grandfather. He believed that nobility showed itself not in acts of war but in patronage of the arts. During his reign, fine buildings became the main outlet for baronial competition. Men who could design them

*John, Fifth Lord Lovel, the builder of the castle*

were highly valued by the king and his barons.

One of these was William of Wynford, a Somerset man who was employed for much of his life on royal building projects. William would have been familiar with the newest fashions in England and France. He may have designed Old Wardour for Lord Lovel.

Portraits of medieval noblemen are rare. It is significant that the only portrait we have of John Lovel shows him not as an armed knight but as a patron of the arts, receiving from an artist a richly illustrated book which he presented to Salisbury Cathedral.

## FRONT DOOR AND ENTRANCE-PASSAGE

The ground level round the house was greatly altered in the eighteenth century. In the Middle Ages, it sloped away much more steeply on either side, so that Lord Lovel's house stood on the end of a low ridge of land.

Unusually, there is no evidence to suggest that the approach to the main door was protected by a ditch crossed by a drawbridge. However, between the towers, up at the level of the battlements, are the remains of a projecting gallery which allowed the entrance to be defended from above in case of attack.

*Right: one of the two pairs of shell-headed seats added by Matthew Arundell on either side of the main entrance*

*Below: Sir Matthew Arundell celebrated his recovery of Old Wardour by adding, above the main doorway, the carved bust of Christ, a raised Arundell coat-of-arms and a Latin description of his work*

The medieval arrangements were swept away by Sir Matthew Arundell's alterations in the 1570s, when the demands of security were less and fashions had changed. Sir Matthew ordered the fronts of the towers on either side of the entrance to be cut back, probably on the advice of a rising architect called Robert Smythson. The narrow medieval windows were made more symmetrical and widened to let in more light. A final flourish was the entrance doorway, which was re-designed in the new Classical style with two shell-headed seats on either side. Over the door is a bust of Christ, the Arundell family coat-of-arms and a Latin inscription recording Sir Matthew's work: the date is given as 1578 (see page 27 for a translation).

Inside the entrance, the door to your right led to a Porter's Lodge, equipped with its own latrine. To your left, the broken side wall of the long narrow entrance passage reveals a cellar that would originally have been concealed from view.

Overhead, the roof of the passage is a modern repair. It is clear that originally the passage was elaborately vaulted in what was – for the 1390s – a very advanced decorative style. It may well have been brightly painted to emphasise the wealth and taste of the Lovel family.

When first built, the narrow entrance passage was defended by a pair of doors and a sliding portcullis at each end. Smythson removed the outer portcullis, but the grooves for the other one can still be seen in the sides of the inner archway which leads into the central courtyard.

## THE CENTRAL COURTYARD

Until the seventeenth century, when the south-west side of the house was blown out in an explosion, the central courtyard would have been a darker and more claustrophobic place. On all six sides, buildings rose to a height of four or five storeys. Most of the original medieval doors and windows were altered in the 1570s, but there are sufficient traces for us to be able to work out what they looked like.

In the centre of the courtyard was a well. Evidence from other castles and palaces suggests that it would have been covered by an elaborate roof. This would have been carved

*Left: reconstruction drawing of the inner courtyard in the Middle Ages by Philip Corke*

*Below: the doorway from the courtyard to the Great Hall staircase*

and painted with the emblems and heraldry of first the Lovels and later the Arundells, emphasising their ancestry and their wealth.

The ground-floor rooms around the courtyard were used mainly for storage and would not have concerned important visitors. They would have been escorted up the elegantly vaulted stair in the corner to the Great Hall on the first floor, its position identifiable to all by the tall windows with their stone tracery and coloured glass.

The doorway to the Hall stair was redesigned in the 1570s as part of Sir Matthew Arundell's refurbishment of the medieval house. It echoes a Roman triumphal arch, emphasising the importance of the approach to the Great Hall. Brightly painted, perhaps in red, green, black and gold, its Italianate design would have provided a dramatic contrast to the Gothic windows of the Hall and the fashionable Elizabethan clothing of those who lived and worked here. It was an extravagant work and Sir Matthew must have been very proud of it.

*Please climb the stair that leads to the Great Hall.*

## THE GREAT HALL

At the top of the stair from the courtyard, medieval visitors would have found themselves in a passageway. On their right, two doors closed off the kitchen and service rooms. Straight ahead, another door closed off a stair going up to private rooms on the upper floors. To their left was a

*Right: the change in level of the carved cornice in the far (north-west) corner of the room allowed for the raised platform on which Lord Lovel's table was placed*

*Below: reconstruction drawing of an Elizabethan banquet in the Great Hall of the castle, by Philip Corke*

wooden screen with arched openings leading into the Great Hall.

*Walk on into the Hall.*

This high room was the formal heart of the house. On feast-days and other special occasions, the whole household would meet and eat here.

On either side, rich fabrics hanging from the carved cornice would have concealed the doorways

leading to winding machinery for the two portcullises which protected the entrance passage below. At the end furthest from the entrance, the carved cornice rises higher to allow for a raised wooden platform. Here, below an embroidered 'canopy of state' and close to the great fireplace, Lord Lovel would come to sit in splendour.

In the 1570s, Sir Matthew Arundell refurbished this great room. The fireplace was reshaped and small square fixing-holes in the walls show that wooden panelling replaced the earlier wall hangings. A row of larger holes for wooden joists in the end wall, above the doorways to the service rooms, shows that a new musicians' gallery was built above the wooden entrance screen. The doorway leading into a lobby behind the Hall was also redesigned. On the other hand, the tall windows were left untouched and

it seems likely that the old wooden roof was similarly left in place.

This may have been simply a matter of cost. However, it may be that while Sir Matthew was anxious to display his awareness of the new fashions, he was also concerned to preserve the aura of knightly chivalry of Lord Lovel's great house.

The sloping grooves cut into the walls at each end of the hall were for a

modern roof, inserted long after the original roof and floor of the Hall had collapsed.

*Walk through the highly decorated doorway at the end of the Hall.*

## THE LOBBY

This narrow room may originally have been no more than a corridor connecting the rooms adjoining the Hall with other more private rooms in the North Tower. On occasion it may also have served as an ante-room to the Great Chamber. However, it was common in the later Middle Ages to use small rooms like this to entertain guests with sweetmeats after the meal while the tables in the Hall were being cleared away for dancing. This association of sweetmeats and 'dis-serving' lies behind the modern word 'dessert'.

In the 1570s Sir Matthew Arundell had the room fitted with new fireplaces. He had the stair in the North Tower altered at the same time to give a more imposing and more private approach to the upper rooms.

*The former stair to the North Tower is now a dead-end. Walk through the other doorway into the Great Chamber.*

## THE GREAT CHAMBER

This room, and the one which lay next to it, formed the main reception suite of the house and must have been sumptuously decorated. Here Lord Lovel (and later Sir Matthew

*Left: the huge fireplace in the Great Hall*

*Left: the doorways at the south-east end of the Great Hall leading to the buttery and pantry*

*Right: ladies in the Great Chamber of a French medieval castle*

BRITISH LIBRARY (Harley 4431 l3)

*Below: the fireplace in the Great Chamber at Old Wardour*

Arundell) would receive favoured guests. On most days they would also dine here while their households ate beyond in the Great Hall. In the privacy of their Great Chamber, their meals were served with the formality appropriate to their status.

Two tall windows in the outer wall looked out towards the gardens and fishponds, while to the left of the brick-lined fireplace a third window (now blocked) looked into the central courtyard. Below it, a

doorway (also blocked) led out into the courtyard – perhaps there was once a wooden gallery there. In the far corner of the room a short passage leads to a latrine.

This room (or perhaps the one above) may have been the one with what was described as an 'extraordinary chimney-piece, valued at £2,000' made of dark marble from a quarry at Cataclews near the Arundell family home in Cornwall. In 1643 it was vandalised by Parliamentarian soldiers who 'did utterly deface and beat down all the carved work thereof with their pole-axes'.

The room beyond was destroyed during a siege in the seventeenth century. While it may have been fitted out as a formal bedchamber, it was probably used as a 'withdrawing room' for receiving especially important or favoured guests. Round the corner to the right are the remains of a stair leading up to the private rooms on the floor above where – for reasons of security and privacy – the real bedchamber would have been.

## THE UPPER ROOMS

Little remains of the rooms above your head on the second floor. These were once probably the most comfortable rooms in the house. They were high rooms with impressive wooden roofs like the Hall. The layout was probably much the same as in the reception suite where you are now, each room having two tall windows looking out over the landscape and a third looking into the courtyard.

The 1605 inventory of the house notes that one of the upper rooms had by that time been converted to a Gallery – a long room with many windows, common on the top floors of great Elizabethan houses. According to the inventory, an ostrich egg hung in the gallery at Wardour: it must have made an interesting subject of conversation.

## THE CHAPEL

Both Lord Lovel and Sir Matthew Arundell would have required a chapel in their house. It is not clear where this was, but it is likely to have been close to their private chambers and so may have been in the upper parts of the house destroyed in the seventeenth-century explosion. In spite of its eighteenth-century religious inscriptions, the small lobby behind the Hall is perhaps too small to have been the original Chapel.

*This ends the tour of this part of the house. To enter the world of the household servants, walk back through the Great Hall and go through the left-hand door at the far end.*

*Reconstruction drawing by Terry Ball of the chapel in the gatehouse at Etal Castle, Northumberland. The chapel at Old Wardour may have been similar*

# ❖ EATING AND DRINKING ❖

Originally, medieval lords ate in the Hall at the head of their households. When Old Wardour was built this still happened at Christmas and the other great feasts, but at other times noblemen expected to eat in their Great Chamber.

There were two formal meals in the day – dinner at about 11 in the morning and supper at 5 in the evening. The Yeoman of the Cellar, the Yeoman of the Buttery and the Yeoman of the Pantry would prepare the table and set up the display of gold and silver plate, bowing respectfully to the empty chair where their lord would eventually sit. Gentleman servants then went through the Hall to the kitchen to collect their lord's food. On the way back, the procession was led by the senior officers of the household.

Only when the food was on the table in the Great Chamber would the lord himself arrive. After his hands had been washed and he had sat down, those guests worthy of eating with him would be seated in the order of their status. The rank of each person was echoed by the rank of the servants who waited on him. All the servants were men. The meal was eaten in silence and the lord was served at least twice as much food as anyone else, even though much of it was carried away afterwards to be given to the poor: these were marks of his nobility.

Food was served in three courses, each made up of a variety of sweet and savoury dishes, and accompanied by dry, sweet and spiced wines. One early fifteenth-century menu suggested boar, beef, mutton, pork, venison, pheasant, swan and capon, followed by an elaborately-sculptured piece of confectionery, as the first course. This was to be followed by more venison, rabbit, peacock, partridge, plover, sea bream, honeyed cake and an even more elaborate piece of confectionery. The third course included curlew, quail, jellied perch, crayfish, baked quinces, sage fritters and cream of almonds. The final confectionery was expected to draw gasps of wonder from everyone present.

*The Duc de Berri, builder of the Palace of Concressault, at table with guests*

## THE SERVICE ROOMS AND OFFICIALS' LODGINGS

### The Buttery

This unheated room, connected by a stair to a vaulted cellar on the floor below, was probably used for serving the beer and ale that was drunk in the Hall. The small square recesses in the walls were fitted with wooden shelves and doors to form cupboards.

Originally the room would have been much darker: the windows were enlarged in the sixteenth century, when security was of less concern. White lime-washed plaster on the walls reflected what light there was. Traces of it can still be seen. All the rooms in the house would have been similarly plastered.

*Walk back into the Hall and then into the next room.*

### The Pantry

This room lay next to the kitchen, to which it was connected by a door and two serving hatches, one of which has been blocked. A cross-wall formerly closed off one end of the room to form a walk-in cupboard within which was a smaller wall-cupboard, perhaps for the expensive spices used to flavour the food. The room was lit by a single narrow window in the back wall, next to the walk-in cupboard.

Here the food cooked in the kitchen would have been dished up, decorated and prepared for ceremonial entry into the Hall.

### The Kitchen

This room had a very high roof to alleviate the heat from cooking. Much of the floor space was taken up by the

*Above: the buttery with its wall recesses for cupboards*

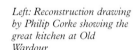

*Left: Reconstruction drawing by Philip Corke showing the great kitchen at Old Wardour*

*The remains of the chimney flue of one of the huge fireplaces in the kitchen. It would originally have been covered by a chimney hood*

huge fireplaces ahead and to your left as you enter. When their chimney hoods were still in place, supported on great stone arches, there would have been much less space to work in.

To your right as you enter was a walk-in cupboard and a stair leading up to a small store-room with shelved wall-cupboards. A later opening allowed rather inconvenient access to the musicians' gallery over the screen passage in the Hall.

Beside the larger fireplace can be seen the remains of down-chutes taking rainwater from the lead roof to storage cisterns in the cellars. Two bread-ovens flanked the hearth.

The window in the arched alcove is a later alteration: the alcove itself seems to have been built to take a lead-lined tank or sink. The door leading through the back of one of the fireplaces is another later alteration. Originally, there was no access from

the kitchen to the guest accommodation in the room beyond.

This great kitchen would not have been used all the time, but only when the house was full of guests. At other times, and especially when the lord and his family were away from home, food was probably cooked in the smaller kitchen on the ground floor below this one. All the kitchen staff would have been men: female domestic servants were uncommon in the Middle Ages.

*Walk back into the Hall again and climb the stair to your right to see the chambers above the service rooms.*

The chamber on the second floor, immediately above the buttery and pantry, was heated but not provided with a private latrine. At some date a doorway was cut through an arched alcove in the inner wall, allowing the occupant to step out onto the musicians' gallery overlooking the Hall. This room may therefore have been allocated to the Clerk of the Kitchen so that he could keep an eye on all the arrangements for cooking and serving the food. Some of his possessions were worth locking up, for there are two small wall-cupboards.

*Carry on up the stairs until you reach the third floor.*

Above, on the third floor and so further from the noise and smell of the kitchen and service rooms, was a grander apartment. This had a large main room and a smaller bed-chamber. The main room was heated by a fireplace in the corner and there was a recess – probably for a latrine – between the two windows. It may have been occupied by a senior household officer such as the Steward or Comptroller of the household.

*Continue up to the fourth floor.*

Above again, on the top floor of the house, was another two-room apartment, heated and with a private latrine like the one below, though here the latrine recess is in the corner. This apartment has lost its lead-covered timber roof and is now open to the sky, allowing views down into the kitchen or out over the surrounding landscape.

From the window in the small bed-chamber, you can see New Wardour Castle, built for Henry,

eighth Lord Arundell, as a replacement for Old Wardour. The family moved there in 1776 – more than a century after the great medieval and Elizabethan house had been made uninhabitable by the damage done during the Civil War.

*Above: the chamber on the third floor*

*Below: the distant view of New Wardour Castle from the top floor of the ruins of Old Wardour*

*Go back onto the stair, looking up to see the remains of the small carved vault at the top, before descending to the Great Hall. From here there are two ways out – down the main stair, or back into the Buttery and down the stair into the Cellar and out into the courtyard.*

## STORE ROOMS AND LODGINGS IN THE COURTYARD

The vaulted room below the long windows of the great Kitchen has been altered several times. The large fireplace suggests that at one time it served as a second kitchen. It was probably used on its own when there were only a few people in residence, and in combination with the main kitchen on the floor above when catering for a large number of people.

Behind the metal grille in the corner was a small cellar. This seems to have been a delivery room for goods carried along a service tunnel running below the gardens from

*The remains of the vaulted ceiling in the room below the great kitchen*

outside the main castle wall. Such tunnels are unusual since they were a potential weakness in a castle's defences: this one may be one of Sir Matthew Arundell's alterations. In 1643 a threat to detonate a gunpowder-mine in this tunnel led to the surrender of the castle.

Across the courtyard, to the left of the entrance passage, were more vaulted store rooms. From these a long passage runs past an external door (cut through the wall in the sixteenth century) and on to a stair which leads up to the Hall. This may have been for carrying wine to Lord Lovel's table in the Hall or to his Chamber. Originally, the stair led on up to the rooms above the main reception suite, but it was later blocked by Sir Matthew Arundell in order to make the upper rooms even more private.

The rooms on the side of the courtyard opposite the entrance passage were almost entirely destroyed in 1644. These seem to have been comfortable apartments for guests. The ground-floor apartments each had their own door: the upper apartments were reached by stairs, one of which survives in the corner of the courtyard beside the lower kitchen.

Each apartment contained two or more large rooms and was provided with a fireplace and a private latrine. The apartments on the top two floors may have been reserved for the most important guests, since here – beyond the reach of enemy ladders – the

*Left: the back of Old Wardour Castle, severely damaged in 1644 during the Civil War*

rooms could have large south-facing windows looking out over the gardens and the park.

*Walk out through the ruined south side of the house, then turn to look back at the damage done in the Civil War.*

## OLD WARDOUR AS A RUIN

By the time of the Civil War, Sir Matthew Arundell's alterations had removed many of Old Wardour's original defensive features. Also, the science of war itself had moved on. Forts were now built low to the ground and cushioned with earth to absorb the impact of cannon balls. The high stone walls of Old Wardour made an easy target. However, while the outer courtyard of the castle was apparently quickly over-run, the massive walls of the house itself proved a tougher obstacle than had been thought.

Ironically, it was the relative luxury of the domestic apartments on the south side of the house that led to its undoing. A drain tunnel led from the many latrines in this part of the house down to the lake outside the castle wall. A gunpowder-mine was detonated in this tunnel, close to the foundations of the house. It shook the structure just where it was most weakened by windows, wall passages and latrine shafts. A large part of the upper floors collapsed, bringing down part of the lead roof and two of the elegant corner turrets.

Not all of the house was made uninhabitable by this collapse, but the most comfortable part was damaged beyond easy repair. In the end, the Arundell family decided not to rebuild it but to move elsewhere.

*Walk on down the slope to the small Banqueting House overlooking the lake.*

*Above: the remaining carved corner turret. The others were destroyed during the Civil War*

*Above: the mock-Gothic Banqueting House in the grounds of Old Wardour, built at the end of the eighteenth century*

*Right: a stained-glass window inside the Banqueting House*

## THE BANQUETING HOUSE

Having been forced to abandon Old Wardour in 1644, the Arundells returned in the 1680s to build a new, smaller house just outside the castle wall. It was to be almost 100 years before they built and moved into New Wardour a little distance away. In the meantime, the family began to develop the grounds around the Old Castle, and the Banqueting House was part of this plan (see panel on pages 20 and 21).

The Banqueting House was built in about 1773–4 in the mock-Gothic style fashionable at the time, as somewhere for the Arundells to entertain their guests.

The building may have been designed by James Paine who was to design New Wardour House. It had a coloured marble fireplace brought from the smaller house. The coloured glass in the windows may have come from New Wardour itself when the chapel there was refurbished in 1786.

A little further along to the east, a three-seater 'necessary house' was also built with detailing similar to that of the Banqueting House. This is also open for visitors to see inside.

By the 1830s, when the grounds of Old Wardour were open to the public, the Banqueting House had become a public refreshment and dining room. The attendant and her kitchen occupied the basement where the public toilets are today.

*Please note that the nearby house outside the castle wall is private property.*

*From the Banqueting House you can follow in the footsteps of eighteenth-century visitors, walking up the slope and passing round the right-hand side of the old house to reach the Grotto.*

## THE GROTTO AND STONE CIRCLE

The Grotto and Stone Circle were the last additions to the romantic landscape at Old Wardour. The Grotto was built in about 1792, by Josiah Lane of Tisbury, a well-known local builder of garden ornaments, who had built other grottos in the area. He was commissioned to create the artificial cave complete with dripping water, fossils and ferns from brick, plaster and stones from Old Wardour itself.

*Facing the grotto, turn left and take the overgrown path to your right around the back of the ticket office, where you will see the Stone Circle.*

This bizarre piece of garden architecture, now barely recognisable as the miniature 'Stone Circle' it was designed as, can be found hidden in the trees behind the Ticket Office, to

the north of the Grotto. It was created by moving the stones of a 4,000-year old stone circle from nearby Tisbury and adding two rustic alcoves which reuse decorative details from the castle and fragments of stucco. Its aim was to simulate an ancient stone circle and to add a touch of prehistoric barbarism to the new landscape. It is now almost lost among the rhododendron bushes at the end of a yew-lined terrace.

*Above: the Grotto, made from bits of the ruined castle in 1792*

*These two rustic alcoves, built in the late 18th century from fragments of the castle, were part of an elaborate garden scheme which included parts of a prehistoric stone circle, brought to Wardour from nearby Tisbury*

# ❖ THE ROMANTIC LANDSCAPE AT OLD WARDOUR ❖

In the later eighteenth and early nineteenth centuries, poets and painters influenced by the Romantic and Picturesque movements in art were fascinated by wild landscapes untamed by man. While the public were being introduced to a world of mountains, waterfalls and caves, archaeologists were discovering the bones and burial urns of long-dead communities, and explorers were encountering primitive peoples in the Americas and Pacific islands.

For those living a life of wealth and luxury, there was an attraction for peoples and past ages uncorrupted by the evils of civilisation, and it was fashionable to incorporate allusions to this idea in buildings and landscapes.

When Henry, eighth Lord Arundell, began to build New

*'Miss Templeton, Mr Holworthy and Miss Crewe sketching in a wooded landscape', a watercolour by James Holworthy (1781–1841). Such painters would have enjoyed the Picturesque qualities of the landscape at Old Wardour*

Wardour in 1769, he had already begun to develop the landscape surrounding the Old Castle as a pleasure ground for the new house. The new landscape was already provided with its main attraction – a genuine medieval ruined castle. Ruins were very popular in Picturesque landscapes. They were a romantic reminder of the world of medieval knightly chivalry, and a place where natural decay could be allowed to take hold and vegetation to grow wild.

The Banqueting House was the next vital component. Here the Arundells and their guests could be served refreshments while contemplating the ruins of the old castle. A short stroll would take them round to the even 'older' Grotto and Stone Circle.

These elements had to be manufactured. The stones for the Stone Circle were brought from a actual 4,000-year old Stone Circle nearby, and were meant to induce a fashionable shudder at the thought of prehistoric barbarism.

The Grotto was the centrepiece of the theatrical fantasy, intended to depict an even more remote era. Here, at the furthest extreme from the elegance of the Banqueting House, the enquiring visitor could encounter nature apparently unchanged by man!

The landscaped pleasure ground of New Wardour thus contained all the necessary elements of a fashionable late eighteenth-century Romantic Landscape. The passage of time, the frailty of human life and the futility of human endeavour could safely be contemplated here before strolling back to New Wardour House for dinner.

*Print of an engraving of Old Wardour from Cattermole's 'Illustrated History of the Great Civil War'*

# HISTORY OF THE CASTLE

The manor of Wardour, which John Lovel acquired some time around 1390, was by no means a large or wealthy estate. At the time of William the Conqueror's great Domesday survey in 1086 it was assessed at about 120 acres. This may have been a deliberate under-assessment for tax purposes, but even so, the manor needed just a single plough-team and it possessed only tiny amounts of meadow, pasture and woodland.

At a much earlier time Wardour had belonged to the kings of Wessex. Alfred the Great once gave judgement on a dispute 'while he stood washing his hands in the chamber there'. By the time of the Norman Conquest, however, the little estate had been given as an endowment to Wilton Abbey, a Benedictine nunnery some 16km (10 miles) away.

Throughout most of the thirteenth and fourteenth centuries, the abbey's tenants at Wardour were the St Martin family. When Sir Lawrence de St Martin died in 1385, he left Wardour to a grand-nephew who was related by marriage to John and Maud Lovel. By what process Wardour passed to the Lovels is not clear, but by 1393 John, fifth Lord Lovel, was in full possession, for in that year he sought and received the king's approval to build a castle there.

## THE LOVEL FAMILY

By the 1390s the Lovel family had acquired land in Northamptonshire, Norfolk, Suffolk and Wiltshire, in addition to Oxfordshire, where they

*Minster Lovel, the ancestral home of the Lovel family in Oxfordshire*

had held land since the twelfth century. Their rise to national prominence came with John Lovel's marriage to Maud Holand, an heiress whose cousins were the half-brothers of Richard II. Through his wife's relations, John Lovel thus found himself in contact with the royal court. Two generations later, the family had risen to become one of the richest in the land.

We do not know why Lord Lovel decided to build a new house here at Wardour. Admittedly, his house at Tichmarsh in Northamptonshire was in disrepair at this time, but he had other houses in Norfolk and Suffolk as well as the ancestral home at Minster Lovel. Whatever the reason for his choice, the outcome was an architectural masterpiece.

## LATE FOURTEENTH-CENTURY POLITICS AND SOCIETY

The late fourteenth century was a time of disruption and suffering for most people. The economy was badly hit by labour shortages as a result of the Black Death, which struck four times in 50 years; people were losing faith in the bishops and priests of an increasingly corrupt church; and the heavily taxed farmers and traders were incensed at the failure of the nobles to bring the war in France to a successful conclusion. Peasant revolt was a constant threat.

England, in common with France and Italy, lapsed into a general uneasiness and despondency. Those who could afford it retreated into a closed world of luxury and self-indulgence, enjoying fine buildings, fanciful clothes and exquisite possessions.

The personal interests of the new king, Richard II, lay with patronage of the arts rather than with warfare. His efforts to end the war with France meant that English and French nobles crossed back and forth between the two countries, engaged in prolonged negotiations. As a result of these contacts, Richard's court became one of the most brilliant and sophisticated in Europe.

*Above: the Black Death killed thousands of people in the 14th century. This is a depiction of the Black Death by an artist in about 1500*

*Below: the marriage of Richard II and Isabella, daughter of King Charles VI of France, in 1396. Isabella was seven years old at the time*

BRITISH LIBRARY (Harley 4380 I89)

BRIDGEMAN ART LIBRARY

*Right: a 1570s carving at the base of the door frame leading from the courtyard to the Great Hall stairway*

This was the world into which Lord Lovel had moved. To show that he really belonged to it, a fine new house in the French style was essential. The inspiration for Old Wardour may have come from a hexagonal palace built by the Duc de Berri, the brother of the French king, at Concressault in central France. The English nobles charged with negotiating a marriage between Richard II and Isabella, the daughter of the French king, Charles VI, and niece of the Duc de Berri, might have visited her uncle's elegant new residence at Concressault.

Wherever the idea came from, it must have taken a remarkable builder to turn it into stones and mortar. Here again Lord Lovel's new connections came into play. Richard II, and the nobles who competed for his attention at court, had attracted and

encouraged a group of experienced master-masons, men whom we would now call architects. Exactly who it was who designed Old Wardour for Lord Lovel we may never know. The best current suggestion is that it was William of Wynford, a former royal builder of West Country origin. Some of the detailing at Old Wardour looks very much like William's work.

Old Wardour is one of three baronial castles built at this time in this area. Nunney, near Frome, was built 20 years earlier for Sir John

*Bottom right: Farleigh Hungerford Castle in Wiltshire, and Nunney Castle in Somerset (opposite), were built at about the same time as Old Wardour. Minster Lovel, Nunney and Farleigh Hungerford are all in the care of English Heritage and open to the public*

de la Mare, who had spent much of his career fighting in France: it is also in the French style. Very different is Farleigh Hungerford, near Trowbridge, built for a lord who came from much humbler origins than Lord Lovel, did not serve in France and had no close connections with the royal court.

Farleigh is much less sophisticated than either Nunney or Old Wardour. Indeed, it looks positively old-fashioned for its time. Perhaps it was only the really rich and assured lords who chose to try out daring new architectural designs: elsewhere, those who had only recently risen to lordly status may have preferred to build something which looked more familiar and more like the type of castle to which their fathers and grandfathers had aspired.

## NEW OWNERS AT OLD WARDOUR

John Lovel, the first owner of Old Wardour, died in 1408. His wife Maud survived him and lived on until 1423, and it was their grandson William who inherited the castle and park. William died in 1455, having in the meantime rebuilt the old family home at Minster Lovel in Oxfordshire.

William's son, another John Lovel, took the Lancastrian side in the Wars of the Roses. When Edward of York defeated the Lancastrians and

*Nunney Castle, Somerset, built in the French style*

became king in 1461, the Lovel estates were confiscated. Old Wardour was let out to a series of lords, including the king's brother, the Duke of Clarence, before being finally sold to Thomas Butler, the Earl of Ormond.

In 1499, the Earl sold the property to Robert, Lord Willoughby de Broke, thus unwittingly involving Old Wardour in a bitter dispute between the various heirs to the Broke inheritance. This dragged on until 1547 when one of the heirs sold Old Wardour to a Cornish gentleman, Sir Thomas Arundell of Lanherne near Newquay.

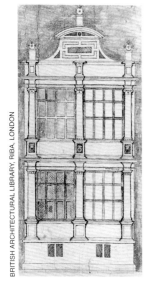

*A drawing, probably by Robert Smythson, for work at nearby Longleat House. It is likely that Smythson directed work at Old Wardour too*

## THE ARUNDELL FAMILY

Sir Thomas Arundell was one of the many men in the Tudor period who made their fortunes by attaching themselves to the households of courtiers. He started in the service of Cardinal Wolsey, Chancellor of England, and managed to escape disgrace when Wolsey fell from favour in 1529. He married a sister of Katharine Howard, and when Katharine married Henry VIII in 1540, he became her chamberlain: a year later he escaped disgrace again when Katharine was accused of adultery and executed. Most of her household gave evidence against her.

Sir Thomas then transferred his allegiance to the Duke of Somerset and rose in wealth and status when his patron became Lord Protector to the young Edward VI. There his ability to escape the disgrace of his benefactors ran out. When the Duke was accused of treason and executed for felony in 1552, Sir Thomas suffered the same fate.

Sir Thomas had used his wealth to buy land and Wardour was one of several properties he had acquired in Wiltshire in the 1540s. All these were now confiscated. Some were later re-granted to his widow and later still given outright to his son, Matthew. The castle and park of Old Wardour was not one of them.

It passed instead to William Herbert, Earl of Pembroke, who – in

one of the ironies of history – now lived nearby in a great house made from the old nunnery of Wilton Abbey, which had owned Wardour at the time of the Norman Conquest.

Matthew Arundell waited for his chance, marrying one of the ladies-in-waiting of the new queen, Elizabeth I. In 1570 he succeeded in recovering Old Wardour from the Earl of Pembroke by an exchange of land. Four years later he was knighted and began to restore what he clearly regarded as family property.

## CHANGES TO THE OLD CASTLE

By the time Sir Matthew Arundell got his hands on the property, Old Wardour would have been regarded as an imposing but uncomfortable and unfashionable house.

Sir Matthew, however, passed over the opportunity to demolish it and build something more in keeping with the architecture of the age. Instead, he decided to refurbish it, taking care to preserve the dignity of the old house while making it more comfortable to live in.

We have no direct record of who was responsible for the work. However, in 1576 Sir Matthew happened to mention in a letter to a friend that Robert Smythson had recently been at the house. This may be significant. Smythson was working nearby at the time, rebuilding

Longleat. He was later to become well known as an architect and designer of great houses, though at this time he was still at an early stage of his long career. It seems likely that he advised Sir Matthew and he may well have directed the work on site.

The restoration which Sir Matthew triumphantly recorded in the inscription above the remodelled entrance included redesigning the doorway to the Hall stair and letting more light into the house by enlarging the windows. The pattern of the windows was also made more symmetrical, with false windows outlined on the outer faces of walls where internal fireplaces prevented real ones being built.

It was probably the private rooms and guest suites in the missing upper parts of the house that benefitted most from the renovation. Here the large south-facing medieval windows may have been opened up even

*Above: the Latin inscription carved over the main entrance of Old Wardour and a translation (left)*

---

# TEXT OF MATTHEW ARUNDELL'S INSCRIPTION OVER THE ENTRANCE TO OLD WARDOUR CASTLE

GENTIS ARUNDELLAE THOMAS LANHERNIA PROLES IUNIOR.
HOC MERUIT PRIMA SEDERE LOCO UT SEDIT CECIDIT.
SINE CRIMINE PLECTITUR ILLE INSONS. INSONTEM FATA
SEQUUTA PROBANT. NAM QUAE PATRIS ERANT
MATTHAEUS FILIUS EMIT EMPTA AUXIT. STUDIO
PRINCIPIS AUCTA MANENT COMPRECOR AUCTA DIV.
MANEANT AUGENDA PER AEVUM HAEC DEDIT. ERIPUIT.
RESTITUITQUE DEUS
1578

*Translation (with thanks to Dr P. Davidson and to Celia Gibbons)*

Thomas, younger scion of the House of the Arundells of Lanherne,
First gained the right to make his home in this place.
But no sooner had he settled than he was executed.
Although he was innocent and above reproach, he was punished.
May his subsequent destiny prove his innocence
(or subsequent events proved that innocence).
For Matthew, his son, redeemed those things which were his father's
And, having bought them, he increased them.
By the favour of the Prince, what he bought/his estate continues to flourish.
May it continue so, I pray, and may it be enriched for ever.
What God gave and took back, He has now restored.
1578

CADW

*The Long Gallery at Old Wardour would have looked similar to the one at Raglan Castle, Monmouthshire, depicted in this reconstruction drawing by Ivan Lapper*

further, and it was probably here that the Gallery, mentioned in the Inventory of 1605, was constructed. The rooms were decorated and furnished in the most extravagant way. The Inventory mentions tapestries and leather wall-hangings; cushions and bed-curtains of silk and velvet; gilded beds and tables inlaid with marble; and as many as 192 pictures – a huge amount for any house at this time. Most of these items were to be looted or smashed after a siege in 1643.

The reason for Sir Matthew's restrained treatment of the old medieval house is not clear. It may have been simply a matter of cost, as well as a desire (as a rich Catholic in a reformed Protestant state) to avoid drawing too much attention to himself. There was, however, a growing fashion for mock-medieval buildings among some members of the Elizabethan aristocracy. Such sham castles were intended to inspire social stability after the decades of political turmoil and to conjure up half-remembered images of baronial chivalry and renown. Something of this may have been at the back of Sir Matthew's mind when he set out to refurbish, but not rebuild, the genuinely baronial house at Old Wardour.

Sir Matthew died in 1598. His son, Sir Thomas, although an ardent Catholic, was created a baron by James I in 1605, the year of the infamous Gunpowder Plot, and so became the first Lord Arundell. His son, the second Lord Arundell, died in 1643 of wounds received while fighting for Charles I in the Civil War.

## THE CIVIL WAR SIEGES AT OLD WARDOUR

When war broke out in 1642, it was perhaps inevitable that the Arundells should support the Royalist cause.

Thomas, the second Lord Arundell, was away from Wardour, attending the king at Oxford, when the first attack came. The defence had therefore to be organised by his wife, Lady Blanche. The garrison at the time numbered about twenty-

*A nineteenth-century print from an engraving, 'The Defence of Old Wardour', showing Lady Arundell and her staff defending Old Wardour during a Civil War siege*

five men, together with Lady Blanche's servants, many of whom were women.

The attack was led by Sir Edward Hungerford, a Parliamentarian commander whose brother held the family castle of Farleigh Hungerford for the King. Such was the nature of the English Civil War.

Old Wardour was hardly a strategic target. It housed no powerful garrison and controlled no important

# ❖ THE ENGLISH CIVIL WAR ❖

In the years between 1642 and 1648, the war between King Charles I and Parliament tore England apart. The differing political, social and religious opinions were so strongly held that they crossed traditional groupings, even splitting families. Members of every social class found themselves briefly allied on one side or the other.

The basic issue was whether the king should rule with the consent of parliament or be accountable only to God. The immediate outcome was the execution of the King in 1649 and the creation of a Commonwealth, later led by Oliver Cromwell as Lord Protector. Yet, by 1660, Cromwell was dead and a new king, Charles II, was on the throne.

The attack on Old Wardour in 1643 was led by Sir Edward Hungerford on behalf of parliament: close by, the family castle of Farleigh Hungerford was held by Sir Edward's brother for the king. The two brothers thus found themselves with opposing loyalties.

The Arundells were both Royalist and Catholic. Sir Edward Hungerford's attack was intended to deprive them of their wealth and enrich his own side, rather than to achieve any great strategic objective. This was the warring of neighbouring lords, much as in the middle ages, centuries before. Neither Hungerford's siege of 1643, nor Lord Arundell's counter-siege of 1644, had any great effect on the outcome of the war.

*A painting by Ernest Crofts dating from 1900, showing Oliver Cromwell at the storming of Basing House. The siege of Old Wardour by parliamentary troops must have been a similar scene.*

*Royalists bring down the back wall of Old Wardour during a Civil War siege. Reconstruction drawing by Philip Corke*

line of communication. Sir Edward's attack was more in the nature of a raid aimed at preventing the Arundells' wealth being used to support the enemies of Parliament.

We do not know what effect Sir Matthew Arundell's renovations may have had on the outer wall and gatehouse of the castle, but it is clear that they severely reduced the ability of the main house to resist attack. By the time of the English Civil War the castle's defences must have been considered very vulnerable.

That the castle was able to hold out at all was due partly to the massive thickness of its walls and partly to the inadequacy of the guns Sir Edward brought to bear on it. For six days his two small cannon made no impact beyond breaking some windows and a chimney-piece. Since the guns were probably placed on the high ground overlooking the entrance to the castle, the broken chimney-piece may have been the one in the Great Hall, where the large graceful windows presented an easy target.

Sir Edward then set off gunpowder mines placed in the service tunnel leading to the cellars of the house and in another tunnel draining the latrines in the domestic suites. The first explosion did little harm: the second probably caused more alarm than structural damage, but was enough to jolt the garrison into surrendering the castle on 2 May 1643.

*Right: signatures on the warrant to execute King Charles I, including that of Edmund Ludlow, who was put in charge of Old Wardour after its surrender in May 1643*

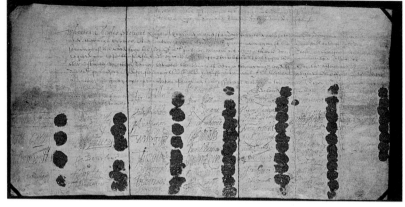

*Below: Charles I, a portrait by Gerard Houthurst (1628)*

Lady Blanche and her children were separated. Her anguish must have been intensified by news of the death of her husband from wounds received fighting elsewhere. The house itself was looted and vandalised, as were the estate buildings and the park. The Arundells later assessed the loss at £100,000, a huge sum at that time.

Parliament placed Old Wardour under the command of Edmund Ludlow, a strong republican who, five years later, was to be one of those who signed the warrant to execute the king. He brought his own troop of horse and a company of infantry – about 100 men in all. It was Thomas Arundell's son Henry, the new third Lord Arundell, who led the Royalist counter-siege in December 1643.

Lord Arundell was supported by professional soldiers and gunners. Cannon were placed on the hill slopes overlooking the main gate, as before,

and the castle outhouses were taken over as observation posts. By the middle of February, several holes had been knocked in the castle walls, more windows had been broken, one of the portcullises had been put out of use and the garrison was beginning to run short of supplies: but that was all.

By 13 March 1644, two gunpowder mines had been laid – possibly in the same tunnel and drain as before. Lord Arundell's intention was presumably to frighten the garrison into surrender: he can hardly have wanted to blow up his own house.

The next morning, however, the vibrations from one of Edmund Ludlow's guns accidentally toppled a burning match into the barrels of gunpowder waiting in the drain tunnel.

The resulting underground explosion was so great that it sent huge cracks up through the structure of the building. Two of the projecting corner-turrets collapsed, bringing down parts of the roof and much of the upper floors of the house.

Edmund Ludlow, who was lying late in bed, found the outer wall of his bedchamber blown out and open to the enemy who attempted to climb in over the debris from the upper parts of the building, which now formed a ramp up to first-floor level. Ludlow fought them off for a while, before crossing to the other side of the room to call for help from his men.

When help came, it was by means of a ladder that was too short to reach the window. What followed would have been farcical if the potential outcome had not been so terrible. Ludlow had to dash back and forth across the room several times, one minute beating off his attackers by the gaping hole in the outer wall, the next minute trying to drag his rescuers in through the courtyard window.

Eventually, with the help of his men, Ludlow was able to barricade the hole in the wall with furniture and turn to the defence of the rest of the house. The resulting stand-off lasted for four days, at the end of which all his food had gone and another gunpowder mine had been prepared. Ludlow was now persuaded by his men to surrender.

Ludlow was led off to prison, but was treated well and was soon freed in an exchange of prisoners. Lord Arundell had his house back, but it was now badly damaged as well as being somewhat old-fashioned. Worse still, the fortune of war in the country as a whole began to turn against the Royalists. With the triumph of Parliament and the execution of the king in 1649, Old Wardour was confiscated yet again as the Arundells forfeited their estates for their part in the war.

## ABANDONMENT AND RETURN

The Arundells eventually recovered their lands but they never rebuilt the ruined house at Old Wardour. Instead, they moved from place to place, spending a good deal of time in London and eventually renting Breamore House in Hampshire.

During the 1680s and 1690s, while at Breamore, the Arundells began to build a new and much smaller house just outside the castle wall at Wardour. It was built from the ruins of the stables and outhouses

*Above: Oliver Cromwell, painted by Robert Walker in 1649*

*Below: engraving of Old Wardour Castle in 1732, by Samuel and Nathaniel Buck*

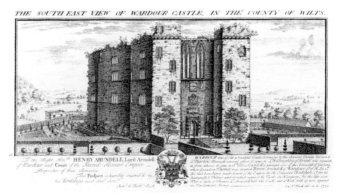

*Above: portrait of Henry, the eighth Lord Arundell*

*Above and right: letter and bill from Capability Brown to Lady Arundell from 1757, relating to work done on Old Wardour*

and part of it still survives within the private residence near the later Banqueting House. Nearby were a brewhouse and a banqueting house, and an orchard was planted in the old Outer Courtyard on the other side of the castle.

The Arundells finally moved all their possessions from Breamore to Wardour and took up seasonal residence there in 1715. Piecemeal additions to this modest residence included better kitchens, a bath house built in the 1720s when cold plunge baths were in fashion, and a new chapel in 1725-6. The orchard was removed in about 1730 and replaced by a garden. This had three terraces with railings and steps and at least one yew-tree alley, overlooking a bowling green. The formal nature of the gardens at this time can be seen in an engraving of 1735 by Samuel and Nathaniel Buck (see page 33).

## NEW WARDOUR AND THE NEW PLEASURE GROUND

All these were swept away when more informal and natural-looking gardens became fashionable (see page 20). The castle and its grounds were now to be the hub of much more extensive schemes. The sixth Lord Arundell began by laying out new riding-paths in the adjoining woodland but he suffered a cash crisis and work came to a halt. In 1754 his son commissioned Lancelot 'Capability' Brown to prepare a more comprehensive scheme, but his death in 1756 prevented anything being done: indeed, Brown had some difficulty in getting paid for his work.

Henry, the eighth Lord Arundell, married a rich heiress in 1763 and inherited further wealth from his mother in 1769. The following year Richard Woods was commissioned to survey the park and produce designs for improvements: these included the proposal for a new mansion two miles away to the north-east. While a substantial amount of work was done to Woods's designs, Lord Arundell found his scheme too expensive to complete in its entirety. However, he did take up the idea of a new house, New Wardour.

New Wardour was designed by James Paine and built between 1769 and 1776. Even before it was finished, Lord Arundell turned for ideas for a better setting to Capability Brown. With some reluctance (entirely understandable, given the delay in paying him on the previous occasion) Brown produced yet another design in 1775. Work went on for three years, but was still incomplete when Brown died in 1783.

By this time the grand design for a lake had been abandoned in favour of several ponds linked to make a winding water-feature. A major achievement, however, was a new Banqueting House built in mock-Gothic style in 1773–4 while New Wardour house was still under construction. It is not clear whether it was designed by Paine himself or left to the landscaper and architect, Richard Woods.

Following the move to New Wardour and the refashioning of the landscape, the Arundells demolished most of the late seventeenth-century house built around and out of the ruins of the old stables and outhouses. What remained was adapted as a farmhouse. It is now a private residence.

By the 1830s the ruins of Old Wardour were open to visitors. The once private Banqueting House became a place for public refreshment and dining parties. The eighteenth-century Romantic landscape, with the great ruined house at its centre, took on a new role as a public amenity – a role which it still plays today.

## LOOKING AFTER OLD WARDOUR

The last Lord Arundell died in 1944, having placed the ruins of the house occupied by his ancestors in the care of the State. Old Wardour is now maintained on behalf of the Secretary of State by English Heritage.

Old Wardour continues to change. The old house and the surrounding parkland are protected by law but nature takes little notice. The landscape designed by Richard Woods and Capability Brown has developed in ways that would have startled them, and the house itself suffers under wind, rain and frost. Almost a third of Josiah Lane's grotto has collapsed.

Looking after Old Wardour is a fight against time itself. The decay of the old house cannot be stopped completely – it can only be slowed down. Conservation and repair are a continuing task, informed by the careful recording and analysis of the building, by the use of scientific instruments to detect what lies below the ground, by careful excavation and by historical research.

Beyond the castle wall, the detailed study of the surrounding landscaped parkland is only just beginning, but it is already clear that it has as much to tell us about the past as the castle itself. Wardour's story is far from over.

*Above: New Wardour House today*

*Below: the coat-of-arms of Henry, the eighth Lord Arundell*

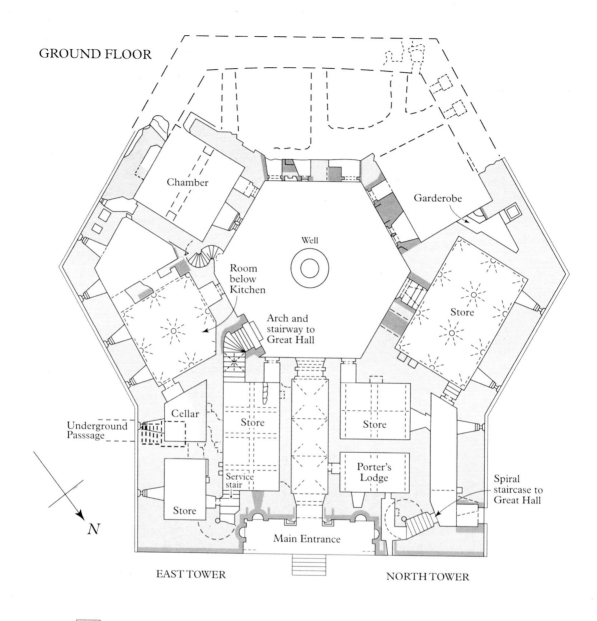

GROUND FLOOR

Chamber

Garderobe

Well

Room below Kitchen

Arch and stairway to Great Hall

Store

Underground Passsage

Cellar

Store

Store

Spiral staircase to Great Hall

Store

Service stair

Porter's Lodge

N

Store

Main Entrance

EAST TOWER

NORTH TOWER

1393: John Lovel's design

1570-78: Matthew Arundell's alterations

Later alterations

| 0 | | 5 | | 10 | | 15 Metres |
|---|---|---|---|---|---|---|

| 0 | 10 | 20 | 30 | 40 | 50 Feet |
|---|---|---|---|---|---|